DANGEROUS DRUGS

HEROIN

KATIE MARSICO

Cavendish
Square
New York

Published in 2014 by Cavendish Square Publishing, LLC
303 Park Avenue South, Suite 1247, New York, NY 10010

Copyright © 2014 by Cavendish Square Publishing, LLC

First Edition

Website: cavendishsq.com

CPSIA Compliance Information: Batch #WW14CSQ

All websites were available and accurate when this book was sent to press.

Library of Congress Cataloging-in-Publication Data
Marsico, Katie.
Heroin / by Katie Marsico.
p. cm. — (Dangerous drugs)
Includes index.
ISBN 978-1-62712-372-3 (hardcover) ISBN 978-1-62712-373-0 (paperback)
ISBN 978-1-62712-374-7 (ebook)
1. Heroin abuse — Juvenile literature. 2. Heroin — Juvenile literature. 3. Heroin — Physiological effect — Juvenile literature. I. Marsico, Katie, 1980-. II. Title.
HV5822.H4 M34 2014
362.29—dc23

EDITORIAL DIRECTOR: Dean Miller
SENIOR EDITOR: Peter Mavrikis
SERIES DESIGNER: Kristen Branch

Photo research by Kristen Branch

The photographs in this book are used by permission and through the courtesy of: Cover photo by Universal Images Group/SuperStock; Universal Images Group/SuperStock, 1; © Ray Grover/Alamy, 4; Christian Martinez Kempin/E+/Getty Images, 6; AP Photo/Rich Pedroncelli, 8; © Bubbles Photolibrary/Alamy, 9; © Sotheby's/akg-images/Newscom, 11; © Antonin Vodak/Alamy, 12; Mpv_51/Bayer Heroin bottle, 12; AP Photo/Mel Evans, 15; Ray Tamarra/Getty Images Entertainment/Getty Images, 17; Frank Micelotta/ Hulton Archive/Getty Images, 17; © Gabriel Olsen/FilmMagic/Getty Images, 17; DEA - digital version copyright Science Faction/Science Faction/Getty Images, 18; DEA - digital version copyright Science Faction/Science Faction/Getty Images, 18; Christian Martínez Kempi/E+/Getty Images, 21; stevecolei- mages/E+/Getty Images, 21; © Janine Wiedel Photolibrary/Alamy, 21; Mikael Häggström/Short-term effects of heroin, 22; Jeff Rotman/Photolibrary/Getty Images, 26; Scott Bodell/Science Faction/Getty Images, 28; image on page 30; © mark follon/Alamy, 32; SW Productions/Photodisc/Getty Images, 36; AP Photo/Donna McWilliam, 40; AP Photo/M. Spencer Green, 40; AP Photo/Mel Evans, 40; © AP Images, 42; © Dennis MacDonald/Alamy, 44; © DCPhoto/Alamy, 47; Jennifer Steck/E+/Getty Images, 51; © Jeff Greenberg/Alamy, 56.

Printed in the United States of America

CONTENTS

CHAPTER ONE

The Most Extreme Drug

MOST YOUNG PEOPLE HAVE HEARD from their teachers or parents that drugs can have harmful—and sometimes even deadly—effects on the mind and body. Yet these words of warning take on a whole new meaning when combined with the life story of someone who has done an illegal and highly dangerous drug called **heroin**. Twenty-six-year-old Tyler of Kentucky knows firsthand how heroin can turn a person's world upside down. He admits that he didn't care much about anything besides getting high once he became **addicted** to the drug. He slept in cars and public bathrooms. He chose

Left: Soon after the initial rush of heroin wears off, users typically feel drowsy and fall into a dreamlike state.

One of the most common methods of abusing heroin involves injecting the drug into a vein.

not to bathe for weeks at a time and shut out the people who truly cared about him.

Tyler initially experimented with heroin as a teenager because he was drawn to the "dark allure of doing the most extreme drug in existence." He had heard that heroin produced an exhilarating rush of pleasure far more intense than the highs associated with other **narcotics**. From what Tyler knew of heroin, it was "bigger, better, stronger, [and] faster acting" than anything else he could try. In addition, all his favorite rock stars used heroin, and it was much cheaper than the prescription painkillers he was already abusing. When he first took heroin, Tyler instantly felt as if he didn't have a stress or worry in the world. He was relaxed, carefree, and totally unaware of what lay ahead of him.

It wasn't long, however, before Tyler needed more and more heroin to enjoy the same pleasant sensations. In his own words, he was "hopeless." He begged, borrowed, and stole to support his habit. Meanwhile, he nearly lost his life on several occasions when he **overdosed** on heroin. Nevertheless, Tyler found it impossible to stop using. From his point of view, heroin didn't just make life better—it eventually became his main reason for living. Luckily, Tyler got help and overcame his addiction in the summer of 2008. But he will never forget nearly giving up everything for the most extreme drug in existence.

Overview of an Opioid

Tyler's story is not uncommon. Few addicts would disagree with his description of heroin. It is an extremely powerful **opioid** that provides an intense and addictive high. Opioids are made from or infused with some form of opium, a juice that comes from the seedpods of certain poppy plants.

Opioids are not always destructive. In fact, some people use them without even realizing it. Doctors often prescribe opioids to patients who have broken a bone or recently had surgery in order to relieve their pain or to help them relax. Yet it is important to remember that this situation

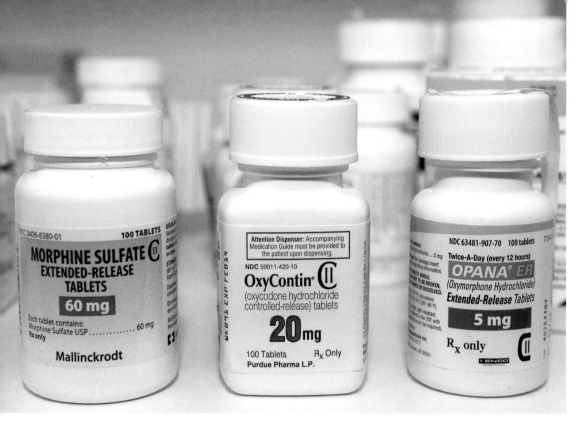

Drugs that are often prescribed to patients for pain relief can become highly addictive if they are overprescribed or abused.

is very different from what occurs when someone abuses an illegal opioid like heroin. For starters, most doctors pay close attention to how much medicine their patients receive and how the drug affects them. Physicians generally do not recommend using opioids for long periods of time or without a good medical reason.

People who abuse heroin are not simply trying to ease their pain under a doctor's care as they recover from an operation for a few days. Most individuals who take this drug break the law and buy it from a dealer. Their goal

8

is to experience euphoria—a feeling of intense happiness or excitement that is often a side effect of opioids. Ultimately, the feelings of pleasure that users first enjoy don't last forever. Nor do they make up for the several dangers that go hand in hand with abusing heroin. People who use this drug face health risks including damaging their internal organs and catching incurable diseases. Sadly, these and other side effects ultimately cost a large number of heroin users their lives.

Sharing needles and reusing dirty needles increases the risk that drug addicts will become infected with diseases such as hepatitis and HIV.

Why would someone tempt fate simply to feel a few moments of extreme happiness or excitement? The answer is that 23 percent of people who start using heroin become addicted to it. They eventually need more and more of the drug to experience the same pleasurable effects. Some users crave heroin, rather the opioids in the drug, after trying it only once. This opioid impacts people of all ages—including kids. In a 2009 survey conducted at the University of Michigan, 1.3 percent of eighth graders in the United States reported having used heroin. Ultimately, the rush that comes from doing this drug is often replaced by the tragedy of serious addiction.

A Less Addictive Option

In about 1810, doctors in Europe began administering what they considered a modern medical wonder. They started using an opioid called morphine to relieve the discomfort that their patients experienced when they were injured or recovering from surgery. German pharmacist F.W.A. Sertürner named the drug after Morpheus, the Greek god of dreams, because users entered a numb and dreamlike trance.

Morphine gained popularity in the United States toward the middle of the nineteenth century. People who used this opioid usually swallowed it as a pill or syrup or injected it into their veins with a needle. The drug became especially valuable when doctors and surgeons treated hundreds of thousands of wounded soldiers during the Civil War (1861–1865).

Morphine, however, also proved to be incredibly addictive. Addicts craved the relaxation and euphoria they experienced once the drug took effect. Doctors knew they had

Ancient Greeks believed that Morpheus—known as the bringer of dreams—was the son of the Greek god *Hypnos*. (Hypnos is the Greek word for "sleep.")

to find a way to help patients who were abusing morphine, but how? Many were hopeful when they heard about a medicine that was being developed in Europe during the late 1800s. By boiling morphine and mixing it with certain acids, scientists believed they had discovered a "safer, less addictive" alternative to morphine. As the nineteenth century drew to a close, US doctors were enthusiastically handing out this new miracle drug—heroin—to patients who were trying to stop using morphine.

During the late nineteenth and early twentieth centuries, people bought small bottles of heroin in over-the-counter kits. These kits typically contained a needle that could be used to inject the drug. Doctors and pharmacists provided patients with heroin cough drops, syrups, and pills.

Over-the-Counter Opioids

In a large number of cases, users were unaware that the opioid was an active ingredient in the medicines they were taking. When they *were* informed, the fact that well-known drug companies were producing large quantities of heroin made the public feel more confident that it was both safe and nonaddictive. It wasn't long before many of these individuals realized how terribly wrong they were.

More Unsafe Than Suspected

It may seem hard to believe, but heroin was just as easy to purchase in the late 1800s and early 1900s as most over-the-counter cold medicines are today. Some patients used heroin in the hope that the drug would help them over-come their addiction to morphine. Others looked to the opioid to relieve a wide variety of medical problems that ranged from the common cough to sleeplessness.

By the early 1900s, doctors started noticing that some of their patients were increasing the amounts of heroin they used taking larger and larger amounts of heroin on a regular basis. Physicians also began to recognize that people who stopped using the opioid experienced several unpleasant side effects. The sleeplessness, nausea, and muscle and bone pain that such users complained of were similar to the withdrawal symptoms that morphine addicts described.

Eventually, doctors came to understand that heroin was an even faster-acting drug than morphine. Addicts quickly grew desperate for the opioid that one user claimed made him feel as if he were "wrapped in God's warmest blanket." In the early 1900s, government officials started passing laws to help control the production and sale of heroin. The Heroin Act of 1924 declared that it was illegal to manufacture or possess the drug. Yet, by that point, heroin had already taken its toll. As of 1925, the United States was home to roughly 200,000 heroin addicts.

ILLEGAL AND HEAVILY ABUSED

Few drugs simply cease to exist just because the government outlaws them, and heroin showed no sign of disappearing. Throughout much of the twentieth century, gangs continued to bring the opioid into the United States after illegally purchasing it in Asia and South and Central America. By the early 1970s, dealers were providing heroin to approximately 750,000 US addicts. More than forty years later, similar statistics were still alarmingly high. In 2011 the National Institute on Drug Abuse estimated that 4.2 million Americans ages twelve and older had abused heroin at least once in their lives.

Buying, selling, or using heroin can result in arrest and imprisonment, but there are several other risks as well. Apart from the serious health issues that addicts face, many have been known to spend between $80 and $200 a day to purchase 150 to 250 milligrams of the opioid. It is not uncommon for such individuals to struggle with problems at school, work, and home as their drug addictions worsen.

14

Ocean County, New Jersey, prosecutor Joseph D. Coronato displays confiscated packets containing heroin.

Some steal or commit other crimes to pay for their habit.

Today, heroin remains the world's most commonly abused opioid. People of all ages, races, and walks of life continue to fall under its devastatingly addictive spell. Many first-time heroin users—including kids—don't realize that a few moments of pleasure often come at the price of a lifetime of pain.

CHAPTER TWO

A Closer Look at a Heroin High

ROBERT DOWNEY JR. HAS SPENT THE past few years earning praise for a variety of film roles, including parts he played in the Sherlock Holmes and Iron Man movies. Nowadays, most people in Hollywood would agree that this award-winning actor is doing quite well for himself. Yet this wasn't always the case. Up until 2003, Downey struggled with addiction to a variety of drugs—including heroin.

"This stuff . . . just grabbed [me] by the . . . heartstrings and tore me apart," he said of heroin during a 2010 interview with *Rolling Stone* magazine. Fortunately for Downey, he got help in time to turn his life around. Not every celebrity who struggles with heroin abuse has been as lucky.

Heroin has played a role in the deaths of well-known actors like John Belushi (died 1982), River Phoenix (1993), and Chris Farley (1997). Famous musicians Billie Holiday (1959), Janis Joplin (1970), Jim Morrison (1971), and Kurt Cobain (1994) suffered similar fates. The list goes on and on, and the question remains: why did performers who demonstrated such amazing talent and promise sacrifice everything for a heroin high?

The simple answer is that drug abuse destroys people from all walks of life, including the rich and famous. When heroin is involved, however, addiction can grip users with remarkable speed and intensity. The opioid

Many celebrities have been affected by heroin addiction, including Robert Downey Jr.(top), Janis Joplin (middle), and Kurt Cobain (bottom).

affects the brain in a way that causes many individuals to lose sight of how much they are risking—and, in many cases, sacrificing—to get high.

Appearance and Methods of Abuse

The appearance of heroin gives few clues that it is a powerful narcotic capable of hooking hundreds of thousands of people, including the celebrities previously mentioned. This opioid often takes the form of a powder that is sold in various shades of brown and white. In some cases, heroin is black and sticky like tar. It goes by a wide range of street names, including smack, junk, tar, snow, and H.

The color and form of the heroin depends on what is mixed into the drug or included as an additive.

Heroin is abused in a few different ways. Some people shoot, or inject, heroin into their veins or muscles. Others swallow, smoke, or snort it. No matter which method is used, heroin rapidly affects how the brain operates.

Scrambling Brain Signals

How exactly does heroin create sensations that make users crave more and more of the drug? The simple answer is that it alters how the body perceives pleasure and pain. Yet the chemical process that triggers this reaction is a bit more complicated.

Whether it is smoked, swallowed, snorted, or injected, heroin ultimately enters a person's bloodstream. Because heroin is the fastest acting of all the opioids, it can reach the brain in a matter of minutes if not sooner. It is then converted, or changed, into morphine, which attaches to the outer surfaces of brain cells known as **opioid receptors**. These cells react by sending out signals that affect the body in many different ways, including altering how a user experiences pain and pleasure. Normally the brain releases natural chemicals called **endorphins**, which trigger opioid receptors in a similar manner. Since heroin causes an increased sense of reward and enjoyment, the

Like many illegal drugs, heroin is frequently mixed, or cut, with other substances before it reaches users.

Common Impurities and Killer Combinations

Sometimes dealers do this on purpose. They blend heroin with everything from sugar to talcum powder. This allows them to sell their drug to more customers and to make a greater profit, since many people do not realize that they are not receiving a pure product.

Yet even dealers aren't always aware of what they are handing out to buyers. It is not uncommon to find traces of gasoline and other poisonous substances in heroin. These chemicals, which are often used to cook narcotics, have been known to pollute the drugs that are being produced.

In many cases, dealers or their customers intentionally mix heroin with other ingredients to create a more intense high. For example, "cheese heroin" is a combination of black tar heroin and crushed over-the-counter medications used to treat allergies, colds, and sleep problems. There is also "speedball," a potentially lethal blend of heroin and a highly addictive stimulant known as cocaine. Speedball caused the deaths of John Belushi, Chris Farley, and River Phoenix.

Television star Corey Montieth died of complications related to heroin abuse.

Short-term effects of
Heroin

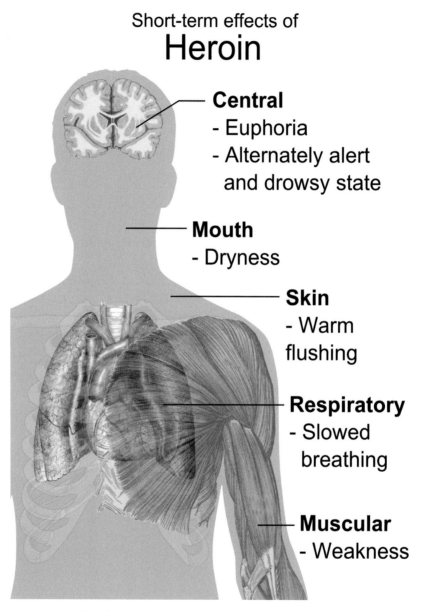

Central
- Euphoria
- Alternately alert
  and drowsy state

Mouth
- Dryness

Skin
- Warm
  flushing

Respiratory
- Slowed
  breathing

Muscular
- Weakness

The diagram above highlights the short-term effects of heroin.

drug takes over the work normally done by endorphins. As a result, the brain slows down its production of endorphins as it becomes more and more **dependent** on opioids to create a feel-good response. Over time, this leaves addicts unable to rely on their own bodies to control pain and pleasure.

Users then turn to heroin over and over again to get high. After taking the drug, a user first experiences a rush of euphoria that generally lasts a few minutes. During this stage, people have reported that their hands and feet seem heavier than usual. Their skin flushes, and their mouths suddenly go dry. Users next slip into a period of deep relaxation for roughly two to six hours. At this point, they are often described as being "on the nod" because they sometimes enter a dreamlike state and even doze off.

While a person is high on heroin, he or she experiences less physical pain and discomfort than normal, not to mention an absence of unpleasant emotions such as fear, anger, and anxiety. Many people describe feeling completely content and in control. Yet these sensations are not permanent. After a while, the effects of the drug wear off, and users are left craving the rewards that their brain has learned to connect with while doing heroin.

Addiction is not the only danger that people face when they try heroin. The brain's opioid receptors are the same parts that control breathing and blood pressure. As a result, heroin users' respiratory systems often become suppressed. This means that they suddenly take deeper and slower breaths. Sometimes people who overdose on heroin stop breathing altogether. Unless they receive medical attention, these individuals can die. Other users fall into comas because heroin suppresses the nervous system, too.

People do not have to be addicts to find themselves in these situations. The first time a person tries heroin could very easily be his or her last if the drug causes the body to shut down. More often, however, users overdose after they have stopped taking the drug for a few weeks but then return to it. They are not always aware that their **tolerance** to heroin has decreased, so they make the sometimes-fatal assumption that they can safely use as much as they did in the past. Tragically, hundreds of thousands of people are willing to risk their health—and, in certain cases, their lives—to chase a heroin high.

CHAPTER THREE

Unimaginable Effect

MOST PEOPLE LOOK IN THE MIRROR before they leave for school or work every day. For heroin users, it is not uncommon to see a complete stranger staring back at them. As their abuse and addiction become more intense, these individuals often start to resemble thin, pale ghosts with sunken, glassy eyes. Sores and bruises frequently coat their arms and legs.

People who abuse heroin often don't care about their shocking appearance. Neither do they care whether or not they go to school or spend time with family and friends. What becomes important to them is the next time they'll be able to get high. Users have reported feeling like every

Long-term heroin abuse takes an extreme toll on users' bodies that is often reflected in their physical appearance.

bone in their body hurts because they're aching for more of the drug. Heroin becomes the only thing in the world that matters to them.

People don't expect to end up this way when they first try the opioid. The effects of abusing heroin take a toll on a person's body, mind, and spirit. They damage relationships and put a user's life—and sometimes the lives of others—in serious danger.

Hard on Physical Health

It's true that some people overdose on heroin and suffer fatal consequences. Yet this drug doesn't always have to kill quickly in order to destroy someone's health. Many of the physical dangers of doing heroin go hand in hand with the way people abuse it. For instance, sharing dirty needles to inject the drug can lead to the spread of

26

illnesses such as **human immunodeficiency virus (HIV)** and **hepatitis**. Injecting heroin has also been known to cause collapsed veins, skin and heart infections, and pus-filled sores called abscesses.

Smoking and snorting are not necessarily safer alternatives to "shooting up," that is, injecting it with a needle. These processes can seriously damage a person's nose, throat, and lungs. Doctors have found that many heroin users suffer from respiratory illnesses such as pneumonia and tuberculosis.

Not everyone who abuses heroin experiences these physical problems right away. On the other hand, the very act of getting high tends to create almost immediate changes in the body. Once users go "on the nod," their nervous system slows down considerably. During this stage of a heroin high, they tend to have slurred speech and visual disturbances. Slower movement, droopy eyelids, and an upset stomach are also common side effects.

Most people find it hard to imagine how they would react if they were told they had HIV or a serious health problem. Yet many of these same individuals don't consider how their day-to-day lives would change if they tried heroin just once or twice. Concentrating on a math

No matter how heroin is taken into the body, it can ultimately damage the lungs, liver, kidneys, and brain. Remember that a wide variety of other substances—including poisonous chemicals—are sometimes mixed

BLOCKAGES IN THE BLOODSTREAM

with the opioid as it is being prepared for sale. Not all of these substances dissolve easily in the bloodstream. Instead, they have been known to cause serious infections when they clog blood vessels that connect to major internal organs. In some cases, the blockages kill off small groups of cells in the lungs, liver, kidneys, or brain.

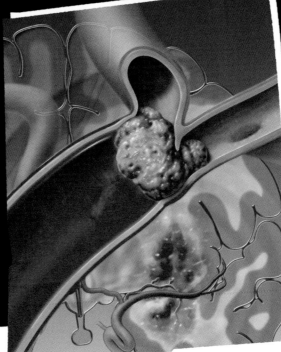

test would be next to impossible without the ability to see straight. How challenging would it be to score a goal during a soccer match with legs and feet that feel as heavy as lead?

These are only a few examples of the unintended consequences of heroin abuse. As many users ultimately discover, this drug affects a person's ability to act responsibly. The choices a person makes while high on heroin can lead to a lifetime of regret—if not the end of life altogether.

The Many Victims of a Blurred Mind

One of the main reasons that people are drawn to heroin is that the opioid alters their sense of reality. It numbs pain and causes them to feel a rush of contentment, comfort, and control. Even after users no longer experience the momentary euphoria that comes from abusing heroin, they slip into a deeply relaxed state that is much like walking through a dream.

The problem, however, is that these sensations are not real. Some people may initially think that tricking their brains into escaping the world is appealing, but it is actually quite dangerous. Ask yourself: Is it safer to cross a busy street awake or half asleep? The answer may seem obvious, but it is less clear to someone dozing in and out of reality on the tail end of a heroin high.

People who abuse drugs like heroin become likely to take risks without thinking about the consequences of their behavior. Being high increases the odds that they will make poor decisions, such as engaging in unprotected sex or committing a crime. While users may tell themselves that they are jeopardizing only their own safety by doing heroin, they are wrong.

The death of eleven-year-old Courtney Sipes is one of countless examples of how heroin abuse can claim the life of an innocent bystander. On November 24, 2009, Courtney was leaving a music lesson in Smithtown, New York. As she crossed the street, an SUV traveling more than 30 miles (50 km) per hour over the speed limit struck and killed her.

Maureen Lambert (above) was under the influence of heroin when she ran over Courtney Snipes.

The driver, twenty-one-year-old Maureen Lambert, fled the scene of the accident. When she turned herself in more than a day later, Lambert confessed to having used heroin shortly before getting behind the wheel of her car. A judge eventually sentenced her to four to twelve years in prison, but no punishment could bring Courtney back. Though Lambert hadn't meant to harm Courtney, her decision to abuse heroin resulted in tragic and deadly consequences.

Harder to Stop Than to Start

Not everyone who tries heroin ends up like Maureen Lambert. Some users get high and never kill or cause harm to another person. However, it is much more difficult to avoid becoming hooked. Is it worth the risk?

Many people realize too late that the intense feelings of a heroin high don't last forever. A lot of addicts start out planning to try the drug only once or twice but end up using several times a day. Along the way, their main focus in life becomes heroin. It takes priority over family and friends—not to mention a successful career, a safe home, and good health.

Sometimes heroin users decide that they want to end their addiction. In most cases, these people learn that they have a long and painful road ahead of them. It is not uncommon for addicts to begin experiencing withdrawal symptoms within a few hours of their last dose of the drug.

In certain situations, heroin withdrawal can prove as dangerous as it is uncomfortable. Doctors usually do not advise addicts to quit without medical help if they have been abusing the opioid for a long time or if they have other health problems. This is because their bodily systems may crash in response to being robbed of heroin. Some long-term addicts who abruptly stop using even have strokes or heart attacks.

KICKING THE HABIT WITH CAUTION

What exactly happens when a person's body is suddenly forced to operate without a substance on which it has become dependent?

Addicts who are going through heroin withdrawal typically suffer from restlessness, depression, and an inability to sleep. They often vomit, have goose bumps, and complain of muscle and bone pain. Some people compare the withdrawal process to an extremely bad case of the flu. These symptoms tend to last for about a week. Nevertheless, they can prove so unpleasant that users frequently give in, give up, and go back to their heroin habit.

It might seem that such horrific side effects would be enough to make anyone steer clear of heroin. Yet heroin abuse remains a serious problem for men, women, and children across the country, and its impact does not stop at individual users.

CHAPTER FOUR

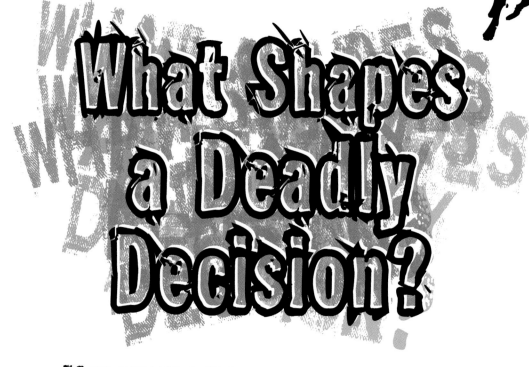

What Shapes a Deadly Decision?

HEROIN IS A VERY REAL CONCERN FOR many communities across the United States. The promise of an intense high lures users to the drug, and all too often traps them in a cycle of addiction. In the process, heroin abuse adds to crime and devastates both small towns and sprawling cities. As a result, concerned citizens are searching for the best ways to spread the word that this drug can and does kill.

"It's not that kids don't understand what heroin can do," notes John Boulihanis, who served twenty-six years with

34

the police force in Melrose Park, Illinois. During his career, Boulihanis saw more than his share of heroin-related arrests and overdoses. "People know some of the dangers, but they're curious. Heroin hits you like lightning. A lot of users are drawn to the idea that 'Nothing else can get hold of me like that.' Unfortunately, once you try it, it's easy to get hooked."

Though some kids are aware that heroin is a powerful and potentially deadly drug, many don't realize how quickly they can become addicted. They are fascinated with the idea of an intense and amazing high and believe that, despite the risks, they can enjoy the opioid without getting hooked. Other users buy into the rumor that heroin is truly dangerous only if it is injected. They are not aware that swallowing, smoking, or snorting the drug can also result in overdose, not to mention a long list of serious health problems.

Another reason that some kids aren't more hesitant to do heroin is that they already have experience with opioids. In 2010, 23 percent of teens surveyed as part of a yearly study conducted by MetLife Foundation admitted to using prescription painkillers that hadn't been prescribed for them. How did they obtain these drugs? Many simply

Many teens head down the road to heroin addiction by abusing
prescription pain relievers.

stole Vicodin, OxyContin, or other pain pills from their parents' medicine cabinets.

Though the chemical makeup of prescription opioids is slightly different from that of heroin, these drugs can produce similar side effects. In a large number of cases, medications prescribed by a family doctor become **gateway drugs**. Kids who savor the rush of opioid abuse are often less timid about moving on from their parents' pill bottles to heroin.

It is also important to keep in mind that not everyone who tries illegal drugs buys them from a street dealer. Some people give in to peer pressure and sample narcotics at a party because they want to fit in. They may also be attracted to the thrill of a drug their friends claim is more glamorous and edgy than commonly abused substances such as marijuana and alcohol. Meanwhile, parents, police, and other community members across the United States are working hard to raise awareness that the consequences of doing heroin are far from glamorous.

From Community Efforts to TV Commercials

Heroin abuse has the power to affect everyone's lives, even if those individuals are not users of the drug. One of the

Is it harder for a person to get heroin or prescription painkillers? A lot of people are surprised when they learn that the answer is prescription medications. For starters, it frequently costs more to buy Vicodin or OxyContin from a street dealer than it does to buy heroin. When purchased illegally, just one prescription pain pill can run anywhere from $40 to $75. Yet a single dose of heroin typically ranges from $10 to $25.

Inexpensive and Easy to Access

In addition, a 2010 study by the National Survey on Drug Use and Health (NSDUH) revealed some startling results about the availability of heroin. Researchers with the NSDUH stated that roughly one in six youths ages twelve to seventeen felt it would be easy for them to get access to the opioid.

reasons that this opioid takes a toll on entire towns and cities is that addiction is closely related to criminal activity. Gangs, prostitution, violence, and property crimes such as burglary often become major problems in areas where many people use drugs. Addicts need to pay for their habit and frequently turn to illegal methods of scoring their next high. Yet this is not the only example of how heroin destroys a community.

On January 28, 2012, eighteen-year-old Megan Miller died in her family's home in Naperville, Illinois. Located west of Chicago, Naperville has nearly 142,000 residents and has earned a reputation for being a safe, family-friendly suburb. In recent years, *Money* magazine declared Naperville to be one of the best places to live in the United States.

Tragically, this description doesn't match the scene that Megan's parents encountered when they entered her bedroom on January 28. The Millers found their daughter curled into a ball and face down on the floor. Megan's mouth was foaming. Three lines of heroin were atop her dresser. Megan was the seventh Naperville resident to die from an overdose on the opioid within a period of thirteen months.

Residents of the suburb were shaken by mounting evidence of a serious heroin problem. They refused to sit

Heroin use and abuse can devastate families. *Top:* Dave Cannata holds a picture of his son Nick Cannata, who died of an apparent overdose of cheese heroin. *Bottom Left:* Brian Kirk poses with his son Matthew's senior portrait and news articles about his death. *Bottom Right:* Marianne Farino sadly holds a picture of her son Raymond, who died of a heroin overdose.

back and continue to allow the drug to claim lives. Shortly after Megan's death, her mother and father spoke to local news networks about their daughter's struggle with heroin. They advised other parents to take an active role in talking to their kids about drugs.

In the meantime, Naperville police held a meeting to spread the word about the realities of heroin abuse. Along with an addiction counselor, they answered residents' questions about the rising number of drug-related arrests and deaths within their community. They provided information about the warning signs of heroin use, as well as the dangerous side effects of the opioid.

The efforts of Naperville residents are just a few examples of how Americans are attempting to deal with heroin abuse. Many communities are working to educate kids about the drug before they try it and become addicted. Local media coverage, school programming, and regular communication with police are all different ways for people to learn exactly how deadly heroin can be.

The fight against heroin occurs on a much larger scale as well. Nonprofit groups like the Partnership at Drugfree.org, formerly known as the Partnership for a Drug-Free America, run national campaigns designed to educate the public about

The ad featuring a woman smashing her kitchen with a frying pan was designed to demonstrate the dramatic and destructive effects of heroin abuse.

teen drug use. The Partnership at Drugfree.org has created or sponsored numerous television ads and websites in an effort to achieve this goal. One such television commercial shows a young woman angrily smashing apart her kitchen with a frying pan. The pan is supposed to represent heroin. The destruction it causes in the kitchen symbolizes the damage that the drug does to every aspect of a user's life.

Whether it's through a television commercial or a conversation with parents or teachers, learning *all* the facts about using heroin can stop someone from making a deadly decision. In the end, people need to think about whether doing a drug that hits them like lightning is worth jeopardizing their future. It's important to remember that if a person gets caught abusing heroin, a police officer or a judge may not give that individual the opportunity to reconsider his or her choice.

Imprisoned for Opioid Abuse

Heroin causes serious and sometimes fatal side effects, but it can also land people behind bars. Since the early 1900s, lawmakers have attempted to crack down on heroin abuse by creating legal consequences for buying, using, and selling the narcotic. Federal laws state that a judge can order a person to spend one year in prison and pay a $5,000 fine for possession of heroin. People risk receiving this sentence even if they have no history of drug use.

State laws that deal with heroin abuse vary in severity, but many are still tough. In certain areas, a state judge can hand down a $50,000 fine and a seven-year jail sentence to a person found guilty of possession. Legal punishments also depend on factors such as how much heroin police discover on a person and whether or not the police believe that any of the drug was intended for sale.

The sale and use of illegal drugs can lead to jail or prison time.

Not everyone who has tried heroin has realized the price they might pay. Many users have sacrificed either their lives or their freedom for a few moments of illegal and dangerous pleasure. Becoming armed with information about heroin helps people make the best decisions possible when it comes to saying "no," seeking help, and figuring out how to educate and assist others.

CHAPTER FIVE

How to Overpower Heroin

MUCH OF THE PUBLIC IS STARTING TO realize that heroin can have a bigger effect on their lives than they ever imagined. Yet people also need to recognize that they are capable of proving themselves more powerful than drugs. They should use what they have learned about heroin to avoid the opioid at all costs. Along the way, they can take steps to help everyone around them do the same.

Be Ready to Refuse Drugs

The odds are good that many people will ultimately find themselves face-to-face with heroin. When that moment arrives, it can be hard to say no—even though it is clear how deadly the decision to use can be. Peer pressure, the desire to try something risky and thrilling, and the need to temporarily escape reality are common temptations. This is why it's important to think ahead in order to avoid tumbling into a cycle of abuse before it's too late.

Since peer pressure is a major reason that kids try drugs, it's a good idea for them to pay attention to who their peers are. Real friends don't try to force each other to do something that might be harmful or dangerous. One simple way to avoid unhealthy peer pressure is to stick with groups that prefer to steer clear of drugs and alcohol. Other tips include not attending parties where guests will likely be drinking or getting high. An alternative is staying close to friends who will offer their support when it comes time to say no.

What if a person experiences peer pressure while trapped alone with someone who is doing heroin? In this case, it's best to politely—but firmly—refuse and leave as quickly as possible. Remember that even being around other people

46

Some teens begin using drugs as a result of peer pressure, while others are attracted to what they imagine will be a thrilling rush.

who are abusing drugs puts everyone in danger of getting hurt or in trouble.

Yet peer pressure may not always be the issue at stake. Some people are attracted to the idea of doing heroin because of its reputation for providing a thrilling physical and mental rush. Luckily, it's not necessary to break the law or risk death to achieve this effect. Playing a sport is a far healthier way to experience intense excitement and an overall sense of well-being.

Most athletic games and competitions also involve a certain amount of risks and rewards. For example, picture a player standing at the three-point line during the last few seconds of a school basketball tournament. Should she pass the ball or try to score? She's taking a risk when she decides to shoot because she knows her whole team is counting on her, and there's a chance she might miss. As she aims for the hoop, her cheeks are flushed and her heart is pounding. Now imagine the surge of satisfaction she feels when the ball swooshes through the net and pounds to the floor mere moments before the buzzer sounds.

The rush that people experience in this situation won't cost them their lungs, heart, or brain. It won't put them at risk for catching an incurable disease or making reckless, irresponsible choices. Athletes may want to relive the euphoria they feel on the court again and again, but their craving won't send them into a destructive downward spiral.

Participating in sports is only one method of achieving a healthy high. Traveling to new places, running in a school election, or performing in a play or concert are a few others. These activities force people to take risks as they work toward achieving a positive goal. The rush of reaching that goal—or even coming close—can offer thrilling rewards without creating life-threatening risks.

If it is life that someone is hoping to escape temporarily by doing heroin, many former addicts admit that they have learned the hard way that it's impossible to run from their problems forever. Everyone feels overwhelmed at times, but people need to realize that drugs will eventually make whatever situation they are struggling with worse. As an opioid, heroin can briefly numb pain. Yet it will not get rid of the reason that a person is angry, sad, or frustrated. Users still eventually have to face whatever issues drove them to try heroin in the first place. Unfortunately, they'll also be dealing with new complications in the form of addiction.

Instead of turning to drugs to drown out problems, people should try talking about their feelings and concerns.

Friends, parents, siblings, coaches, and teachers are all options. So are family doctors and school counselors. Some individuals also find that exercise, music, **meditation**, and prayer help them relax and refocus during periods of stress. Regardless of how tough life may seem, heroin—like any drug—will only further trap users in their troubles.

Overcoming Addiction

It is possible for people to say no to heroin even if they are already hooked. The key is to waste no time getting help. Friends and family members should offer their full support if someone they know is battling addiction. If a person has been abusing heroin for a long time or has participated in risky behavior such as sharing needles, it's also a good idea to be examined by a doctor. Physicians, school counselors, and drug hotlines are all excellent starting points for figuring out the treatment plan that works best for recovering users and their families.

In some cases people find it necessary to stage an intervention in order to convince an addict to get help. During an intervention, family and friends typically work with a drug counselor or health care professional to confront an addict about his or her problem. The point of an intervention

50

is not to scare or to shame a user; it is to encourage the person to participate in **rehabilitation**, or rehab. In most situations friends and loved ones are simply attempting to show their support by helping someone face up to his or her addiction and focus on getting better.

Drug users can often overcome a cycle of addiction with the help of counseling, support groups, and family and friends.

Depending on the intensity of a person's drug problem, rehab may take the form of an inpatient program. This means that patients actually live on-site at a hospital, counseling center, or treatment facility. Inpatient rehab tends to work best if someone is dealing with long-term addiction or an immediate health risk. Doctors and counselors can keep a close eye on former users and help them physically and mentally recover if they recently experienced an overdose or are struggling with especially painful withdrawal. Inpatient programs generally last about thirty days, though some rehab plans run shorter or longer.

Outpatient recovery plans are structured differently. People who do these programs usually continue to live at home. They visit a hospital or counseling center on a regular basis to learn more about their addiction and how to overcome it. Outpatient programs are a good option if heroin abuse doesn't pose an immediate threat to an addict's safety or the safety of others. It's possible that a person may start inpatient treatment and move on to an outpatient plan—which usually lasts anywhere from two to twelve months—when he or she is ready.

Regardless of which path former users choose, medical staff and counselors often help them deal with their drug problem by encouraging them to participate in **therapy**. During therapy, patients explore why they became addicted to heroin in the first place and how they can prevent the drug from taking over their lives again. Certain therapy sessions are private, while others take place in a group setting with fellow addicts. Family and friends may even attend therapy with patients to learn new ways to aid them in their recovery. These types of sessions frequently allow loved ones to open up to former users, so they can reflect upon how addiction has affected their relationship.

Make no mistake, treatment for heroin abuse is hardly ever an easy process. It is true that the urge to use drugs may remain with former addicts for years to come, if not throughout their entire lifetimes. Yet rehab gives them the tools and support they need to make better choices and to work through their temptations.

Educating Others

Learning the facts about any drug, including heroin, is the best way to avoid using it in the first place. Yet it is also important to share this knowledge with others. When people are open about their decisions to say no to drugs,

Watch for Warning Signs

What are the signs that someone might be using heroin? This chart lists several clues that often hint at heroin abuse.

APPEARANCE
- Takes less interest in physical appearance may bathe less often and change clothing less frequently than normal
- Complexion is pale or dark shadows appear under the eyes
- Glassy eyes with small, pinpoint sized pupils
- Unexplained scars, cuts, sores, or bruises on arms and legs
- Red, irritated nose

HEALTH
- Suddenly coughs, sneezes, or sniffles more than usual
- Loses weight without exercising or dieting (heroin abuse can affect one's appetite and cause stomach problems)
- Has infected skin or flesh wounds
- Seems to get sick more often than normal (since sharing dirty needles can lead to the spread of several different illnesses and diseases)

SUSPICIOUS ITEMS

- Burned spoons, foil, bottled caps, or glass tubes
- Straws, glass pipes, or rolled-up dollar bills that have traces of white or brown powder on them
- Needles that someone doesn't need to own for a specific medical reason
- Any unusual powder or tar-like substance wrapped in baggies, paper, or foil

BEHAVIOR

- Slurred speech
- Sleeps more than normal or dozes off during what should be periods of alertness
- Spends less time with family and friends and more time in the company of people who are known to use drugs
- Is caught stealing or abusing drugs
- Shows less interest in former activities and responsibilities at school, work, and home

Teens play a powerful role when it comes to raising awareness about avoiding the dangers of drugs and conquering addiction.

they serve as role models for everyone around them. They make it easier for their peers to say no, too.

More kids need to work with their schools and communities to spread the facts about heroin. One idea is to approach teachers or local leaders about hanging posters that provide statistics on heroin abuse. Posters should ideally include warning signs that may indicate someone is using, as well as contact information for nearby rehab and recovery centers.

Another possible strategy is talking to an adult about inviting experts on heroin abuse to visit schools and community centers. Such individuals might be addiction counselors, police officers, or even former heroin addicts. Ask the experts for their opinions on the best ways to stop Americans from abusing this dangerous narcotic.

Everyone needs to do their parts in spreading the word that heroin is a powerful poison. Understanding what this opioid is and the damage it does can serve as the first line of defense against a painful cycle of abuse and addiction. Keeping others informed is an excellent way to save lives that are at risk of being ripped apart by heroin—the most extreme drug in existence.

GLOSSARY

addicted physically or mentally dependent on a
particular substance

dependent having an intense emotional or physical need
for something

endorphins naturally produced bodily chemicals that
activate the brain cells that control how people
experience pain and pleasure

gateway drugs drug that lead users to abuse even more
dangerous drugs

hepatitis a disease that causes sufferers to have a painful,
swollen liver

heroin a highly addictive and illegal narcotic made from
morphine that causes users to experience euphoria and
an absence of pain

human immunodeficiency virus (HIV) an incurable
virus that attacks the body's white blood cells and
makes it hard to fight off infections; HIV causes a
serious disease called acquired immunodeficiency
syndrome (AIDS)

meditation a mental exercise involving deep thinking and peaceful reflection that increases a person's overall focus and relaxation

narcotics drugs that tend to cause sleep, reduce pain, affect mood and behavior, and prove addictive when used for nonmedical purposes

opioid a painkilling drug that is made from or contains some form of opium (a juice that comes from the seed pods of certain poppy plants)

opioid receptors brain cells that send out signals that affect how the body experiences pain and pleasure

overdosed took such an excessively dangerous amount of a certain drug that the body began to shut down; this sometimes results in death

rehabilitation treatment for drug or alcohol abuse

therapy counseling designed to help a person overcome a negative behavior such as drug abuse

tolerance reduced sensitivity to a substance after repeated use

withdrawal symptoms that occur when a person who is physically dependent on a drug stops using it

Find Out More

Books

Cobb, Allan B. *Heroin.* New York: Chelsea House Publishers, 2009.

Friedman, Lauri S., ed. *Drug Abuse.* Detroit: Greenhaven Press, 2012.

Hollander, Barbara. *Addiction.* New York: Rosen Publishing, 2012.

Marshall Cavendish Reference. *Drugs of Abuse.* New York: Marshall Cavendish, 2012.

———. *Substance Abuse, Addiction, and Treatment.* New York: Marshall Cavendish, 2012.

Websites

Center for Substance Abuse Treatment (CSAT)
www.samhsa.gov/about/csat.aspx
CSAT is a good resource if someone needs to find a local treatment center to help overcome a drug problem.

KidsHealth—

What You Need to Know about Drugs: Heroin

www.kidshealth.org/kid/grow/drugs_alcohol/know_drugs_heroin.html

This site provides additional information on heroin and how it is abused.

Narconon International—History of Heroin

www.narconon.org/drug-information/heroin-history.html

View this page for a more detailed history of how heroin was created and how it became a widely abused narcotic.

PBS Kids Go!—It's My Life: Drug Abuse—Heroin

www.pbskids.org/itsmylife/body/drugabuse/article8.html

Check out this website for more information about how heroin and drug addiction affect a person's health.

Index

Pages in **boldface** are illustrations

About the Author

KATIE MARSICO has written more than 100 books for children and young adults. Before becoming a full-time author she worked as a managing editor. Marsico lives in a suburb of Chicago, Illinois with her husband and five children.